**Essential Question**
Why do people run for public office?

FLOOZLE DREAMS

by
Eirlys Hunter

illustrated by
Cristian Mallea

Chapter 1
Donald Lopskill's Floozle Dreams.....2

Chapter 2
Jana Lopskill's Ideas...............6

Chapter 3
A Great Governor................10

Respond to Reading.............16

PAIRED READ The Job of a Governor......17

Focus on Literary Elements.......20

CHAPTER 1

Donald Lopskill's Floozle Dreams

Donald Lopskill **settled** back into his chair. "What would you like to know, Zane?" he asked.

"I'm doing a school project. I have to interview someone who has an interesting life," I said. "Why did you run for state **governor**?"

The old man smiled and said, "I ran for governor because of the game floozle."

"You played floozle, sir?" I was **astonished**, or surprised. I checked that my hologramizer was working. This interview might be very interesting.

"Yes, I played floozle," said the ex-governor. "And you can call me D.L."

Mrs. Lopskill brought in some iced tea. "Why don't we show Zane some old holograms from our **archive**?" she suggested.

"Good idea, Jana!" D.L. said, and he quickly flicked on a hologram.

"That's me," D.L. said, pointing at number 8. "Then I broke my leg. I couldn't play floozle anymore, but I wanted to help the sport. The governor wouldn't build a new floozle stadium in Astoria, so I ran for governor.

"So you became governor because of floozle?" I asked.

"Yes," D.L. replied. "I dreamed of hosting visiting teams at the Governor's **Mansion**."

"It was a close race," said Mrs. Lopskill, "but he won."

STOP AND CHECK

Why did D.L. run for governor?

CHAPTER 2

Jana Lopskill's Ideas

"I met Jana the year I became governor. We got married," D.L. said. "Jana taught elementary school back then, and she was disappointed her students couldn't use the new floozle stadium."

"Why not?" I asked.

"You had to be 18 to play floozle then," D.L. said. "The jet packs we used for flying were dangerous. Jana **persuaded** me to spend some state money on playgrounds and sports for children."

D.L. showed me another hologram. "That's me at a new playground. The children wanted me to try everything. I had a whale of a time!" D.L. said, chuckling. "Then I found something else that **urgently** needed me."

Mrs. Lopskill explained, "It happened when we stopped for lunch at Lake Astoria one day."

"The lake water was filthy," D.L. said. "We were horrified when we **realized** that the water we drank came from the lake."

Mrs. Lopskill said, "I urged D.L. to have the lake cleaned up."

"And did you?" I asked.

"The lake was dirty because Horace Bumble's factory was polluting it," D.L. replied. "I told Bumble the state of Astoria wouldn't **tolerate** it. I **intended** to close his factory unless he stopped it from polluting the water."

"What did Bumble say?" I asked.

D.L. answered, "Bumble said he could do what he liked. Then he ran against me for governor!"

"What happened?" I asked.

"Well, that got under my skin. I couldn't let an **opponent** like Bumble beat me. I wanted to win a second term as governor so that everyone could have clean drinking water."

D.L. frowned and said, "It was a nasty **campaign**. Bumble told people that I wanted to close every factory in Astoria."

STOP AND CHECK

Why did D.L. decide to run for governor again?

CHAPTER 3

A Great Governor

Mrs. Lopskill said, "D.L. had an **overwhelming** victory. And the lake was cleaned up."

"I was **weary** afterward, but I still worked hard. I set up a chat hour," D.L. said. "People told me about their problems. They could tell me about a school that needed new classrooms."

"He was a great governor," Mrs. Lopskill said proudly.

D.L. smiled. "I loved being governor because I was able to make life better for people."

D.L. said, "I loved it so much that I nearly missed the first Floozle Cup final in the new stadium! I was opening the Renewable Energy Transportation Company. It's famous now for making safe, clean transportation."

"Like my power pack?" I asked.

"Yes! The company **employed** everyone from Bumble's closed factory. That was a great day."

I asked, "What was the best thing about being governor?"

D.L. looked thoughtful. "I liked making sure that the drinking water was clean and creating new jobs. I also learned how important it was to listen to people who had good ideas."

He lifted his iced tea and **saluted** his wife. It was a great place to finish the interview.

I thanked D.L. and Mrs. Lopskill. Then I blurted out, "It's a great stadium, sir! It's my dream to play floozle there one day."

D.L. grinned. "That's wonderful, Zane! What position do you play?"

"I play top flier," I said. "I scored four goals last weekend."

"Great!" D.L. said. Then he stood up and click-clacked his walking stick across the wooden floor to the closet.

"This is for you, Zane," he said. He gave me a ball signed by the Astorian floozle team of 2091, the first winners of the Donald Lopskill Cup!

STOP AND CHECK

What does D.L. believe were his greatest achievements?

Summarize

Summarize why Donald Lopskill ran for office. Your graphic organizer may help.

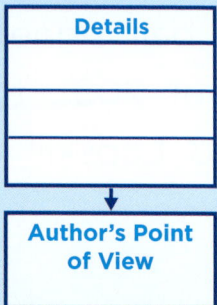

Text Evidence

1. From what point of view is this story told? Use details from the text to show who is the narrator. **POINT OF VIEW**

2. Find the word *position* on page 14. What does it mean? What clues in the text helped you figure out the meaning? **VOCABULARY**

3. Write about how the story would be different if Mrs. Lopskill were telling it. **WRITE ABOUT READING**

> **Genre** Expository Text
>
> **Compare Texts**
> Read more about the role of a governor.

The Job of a Governor

A governor is in charge of a state. The governor leads the state the way a principal leads a school. Governors are usually elected for a term of four years.

Many governors were lawyers before they ran for office. Other governors ran businesses. Governors need to understand business and law.

Nellie Tayloe Ross (1876–1977) became the first woman governor in 1925. She was the governor of Wyoming.

Governors have many responsibilities. They work with the people who pass the state's laws. Governors can sometimes stop a law if they don't agree with it.

Governors also make a budget. Governors decide what to spend money on. They make sure the states can pay for the things that need to be done.

A governor lives in the Governor's Mansion.

The State Constitution

Each state has its own government. A state also has a state constitution. This protects the rights of its citizens.

Governors give a speech every year. They tell voters their plans. This is called The State of the State Address.

It is also the governor's job to go to events and meet important visitors. The governor's husband or wife usually **accompanies** the governor.

You can see that a governor has many responsibilities.

Make Connections

What does a governor do? ESSENTIAL QUESTION

How is Governor Lopskill's work the same as a governor's work in *The Job of a Governor*? How is it different? TEXT TO TEXT

Focus on Literary Elements

Onomatopoeia Onomatopoeia means a word that sounds like what it describes. Animal sounds, such as *woof*, *meow*, *croak*, and *cluck*, are examples of onomatopoeia. They sound like the sounds made by certain animals.

Read and Find The word *chuckling* is used on page 7. It sounds like the kind of small laugh it describes. On page 14, Governor Lopskill's walking stick *click-clacked* on the wooden floor. The words sound like the sound the walking stick makes.

Your Turn

Work with a partner. Think of some examples of onomatopoeia that describe the sounds water makes, such as *splash*.